MW01295435

CONTENTIOUSLY
CONTENDING

A WORD TO TODAY'S

APOLOGETICS EMPHASIS

ANTON BOSCH

CONTENTIOUSLY CONTENDING: A WORD TO TODAY'S APOLOGETICS EMPHASIS

Disclaimer: The Author and Publisher have applied their best efforts to make this book, including all footnotes and quotes, as accurate as possible. In the event that there may be any inaccuracy, this is unintentional and we apologize for such oversight.

All scripture quotations, unless otherwise indicated, are taken from the New King James Version. Copyright 1979, 1980, 1982 by Thomas Nelson, inc. Used by permission. All rights reserved.

ISBN-978-1494764807
ISBN-10: 1494764806

Printed in the United States of America
Published by: Eldad Press, 9070 Sunland Blvd, Sun Valley, CA, 91352, USA
anton@ifcb.net

Photo credit: St Marys on the Hill Stained glass window shattered

First Edition
14 13 12 11 10 / 10 9 8 7 6 5 4 3 2 1

FOREWORD

THIS BOOKLET BEGAN AS a series of articles written in 2007. It was published on a number of electronic forums, particularly on www.herescope.com. I wrote the articles in response to several decades of participation with, and observation of, many apologetic or discernment type ministries. While I see a great need for watchmen who will faithfully sound the alarm at the attacks of the enemy, I also see the need for those involved in this vital ministry to go about this work in a godly way. I am deeply concerned that many who involve themselves in these ministries do so for the wrong reasons and/or with the wrong attitude. In the process they cause more damage than the very error they are trying to correct.

My intention with these humble words is not to discredit or discourage those who sound the alarm, but to exhort such to use the right methods, with the right attitude. I also wish to warn those believers who have become aware of the great deception going on in the Church that a wrong attitude is just as erroneous as wrong doctrine. It does not help if we have our doctrine straight but our attitude does not accord with the Spirit of Christ.

Thank you to Sarah Leslie who encouraged me to write these thoughts down and who has spent many hours re-reading and editing the manuscript in order to arrive at the finished product.

Thank you also to Beatrice, my daughter, who did the layout and who prepared the manuscript of the first edition for print.

I also want to thank Brothers Greg and Shane who encouraged me to make these words more widely available and Brother Greg for help with the design of the color cover and the heavy lifting of getting the second edition published.

COMMENDATIONS

"Through His Word in the Bible God instructs us that we should contend earnestly for the faith which was once for all delivered to the saints (Jude 3). However, we are now living in an era marred by the influence of postmodernism even within the visible church community. Add to this the influx of contemplative mysticism and you have the recipe for an "anything goes" approach to the Gospel which we are now witnessing. As such, people are deciding doctrinal issues by subjective feelings rather than turning to the proper Christian spirituality of sola Scriptura. Pastor Anton Bosch is spot on when he writes: "Experiential theology is wrong when it is based on someone's positive or negative experience and not on the Bible." In my opinion, the clear message shared by Bosch in Contentiously Contending is more needed now than perhaps any time in the history of the Christian church."

-KEN SILVA; PRESIDENT, APPRISING MINISTRIES APPRISING.ORG

"If pride is the greatest sin, then humility is our greatest asset. I found this book to be both convicting and challenging. It should force all of us to ask, 'Lord, is it I'? A must read for anyone in aplogetics ministry."

-SHANE IDLEMAN; LEAD PASTOR, WESTSIDE CHRISITAN FELLOWSHIP, LANCASTER, CA.

"The exposing of deceptive teachings should always be done by assessing them in the light of clearly stated biblical doctrine. Only the truth of God's Word has the inherent spiritual power to enlighten a person's understanding and set him/her free from error. Vain arguments based upon human reasoning and incriminatory remarks will only compound the differences and produce ill feelings which work against a worthy solution rather than correcting the wrongs. In this booklet, Anton Bosch gives sound advice on how to practice biblical apologetics in such a way that the truth will prevail."

-PROF. JOHAN MALAN; CHRISTIAN TEACHER AND AUTHOR (SOUTH AFRICA)

"In the midst of doing the work of God many workers forget the importance of ministering in the humility and love of Jesus Christ to others. We can be so right we are wrong. Brother Anton gives us the Biblical way forward in speaking any corrective word to the body of Christ."

-GREG GORDON; FOUNDER, SERMONINDEX.NET

"I wholeheartedly and unreservedly endorse and commend this booklet by my friend Anton Bosch. We are called to Contend EARNESTLY for THE Faith, but none of us is beyond correction and we should all be open and approachable by anyone in the spirit and attitude of the Bereans. Sola Scriptura is our safeguard and should be our only catch cry. I am concerned by those who "fly off the handle" when they are challenged and by those who fail to correct misquotes when they have been pointed out. This is not the spirit of Christ, which according to Paul is the test of whether we belong to Him – cf. Romans 8:9 with verse 16. Anton has rendered a great service to the Kingdom of God and to the Watchman Ministries world-wide."

- PHILIP L. POWELL; PASTOR, CHRISTIAN WITNESS MINISTRIES FELLOWSHIP (AUSTRALIA)

"Today there are many individuals in the Christian community who will rush headlong into a battle for the truth, but do so in a decidedly unchristlike manner. In writing 'Contentiously Contending' Anton Bosch has done a great service to the Church by reminding us that while we are exhorted to 'contend earnestly for the faith' we are also commanded to do so in gentleness, with a meek and humble spirit."

- GARY OSBORNE; SENIOR PASTOR, BEREAN ASSEMBLY SPRING HILL, FLORIDA

"The topics dealt with in this e-book are most relevant for the serious Christian who wishes to be relevant in today's society. Anton Bosch is a remarkable pastor, teacher and counselor, who not only writes well but is also gifted in applying theological principles in everyday situations with a sense of urgency at a personal and communal level. I warmly commend this e-book to all Christians who take their faith seriously by trying to live out the teachings of the Bible."

- ARTHUR SONG (D.PHIL, M.TH, L.TH -HONS); FORMER DEAN, FACULTY OF THEOLOGY AT THE UNIVERSITY OF ZULULAND

"This booklet wisely and succinctly deals with the work of discernment which is one of the spiritual gifts mentioned in 1Corinthians – more fully described as the 'ability of certain Christian believers to clearly recognise and distinguish between the influence of God and Satan in our world today.' Along with wisdom, and borne up by the safety net of Christ's own nature – i.e., fruit of the spirit – such that are called are essential to the end time church. False teaching and prophecies, even a false gospel are leading many astray – then follows gross apostasy. Be kind when pointing out error and you may be listened to, rather than being wise in your own eyes which turns people away."

- ROGER PALMER; FOUNDER, CHRISTIAN EXPRESSION MINISTRIES (UK)

"This booklet is one of the building blocks of the foundation of my faith. It has often provided me with a standard and plumbline for my conduct insofar as discernment and correction are concerned. It continues to convict me that unless my own heart is one of humility and gentleness I cannot minister to one that I must think of as my brethren. Truth cannot stand alone. Unless it is coupled with love it is not the way of the Lord. Patient, heartfelt prayer must be involved in correction. This booklet literally altered my prayer life when I read it years ago and continues to be a method of correction for me each time I re-read it."

- BARBARA WILHELM; SUNDAY SCHOOL TEACHER AND OCCASIONAL WRITER

"*Contentiously Contending* is a much needed caution and exhortation that helps those who have a true zeal for the truth fight for that truth according to the clear instruction of the Word of God. Just as in Paul's day, some have a zeal but not according to knowledge. In issues like these that are so dear to our hearts, we all have the temptation to think and feel in the flesh and this book is a wonderful tool that God is using to help us escape that snare. I wholeheartedly recommend it!"

- ROD PAGE; PASTOR, LEWISTON COMMUNITY CHURCH

TABLE OF CONTENTS

CHAPTER 1

CONTENTIOUSLY CONTENDING

"Therefore, as the elect of God, holy and beloved, put on tender mercies, kindness, humility, meekness, longsuffering" -COLOSSIANS 3:12

JUDE URGES US "TO contend earnestly for the faith which was once for all delivered to the saints" (Jude 3). Many have found this verse a wonderful excuse to be argumentative, contentious, vindictive, loud, aggressive, mean, nasty and antagonistic as they vigorously pursue all who do not agree with their version of the Truth. But is this really what Jude meant? While Jude makes this statement, he does not elaborate on how we are to contend. For this we need to look at the rest of the New Testament. Some build an entire ministry, and excuse their bad attitude, based on this single word. Doing so is as wrong as any error they may be standing against since they take this word out of the context of the general teaching of the Bible.

Jesus is our prime example, and there is not a single reference to Him becoming vindictive in His interface with the enemies of the Gospel. Even when contending with the Devil in the wilderness He simply quoted the Word in a defensive manner. He never went over to the offense, and He did not resort to calling the Devil names or attacking him personally. Jesus exhibited the same restraint in firmly standing for Truth against the Scribes, Pharisees, and even the Romans (See chapter 5). The reality is that He did not have anything to prove. He was secure in His ministry and mission, and in Who He was. It seems to me that those who take the battle personally, and who resort to malicious attacks on those who believe and teach error, are insecure in who they are and in what they believe, and therefore need to prove themselves by discrediting everyone else around them.

One of the things that distinguished the unconverted Saul from the converted Paul was the aggression of the first and the meekness (not weakness) of the second. He changed from being the pursuer to being pursued, and from the aggressor to the defender. Yes, he never hesitated to defend the Truth and was very forthright in denouncing evil, but that malicious streak was left behind on the Damascus Road. He understood that he was "… appointed for the defense of the gospel" (Philippians 1:17, emphasis mine). The Faith was something that needed to be defended, and not to be forced on those who had no interest in Truth. Is it possible that those who aggressively seek to force their point of view on others have not been converted or are contending in the flesh? There is little difference between such people and the radical Muslim, Nazi or other extremist. It seems to me the attitude and method is the same, it's just the ideology that is different.

Then there are those who use Ephesians 6:17 ("And take the helmet of salvation, and the sword of the Spirit, which is the word of God") as an excuse to use the Word as a dagger and a knife to cut, stab and maim those that cross their path. But this verse gives absolutely no sanction to use the Bible to cut and hurt other people. In fact, the context is clear that the armor is to be used in our struggle against the Devil and his demons, and specifically excludes flesh and blood from the battle (Ephesians 6:11-12). There is no verse in the Bible that gives us the right to use the Bible as a sword against people. Even when contending with Satan, the Sword is primarily a defensive weapon. Anyone who has watched a sword fight or a fencing match on television will recognize that ninety-nine per cent of the time the sword is used defensively to ward off the opponent's attacks. Only rarely is it actually used to lunge or attack.

Remember again how Jesus used the Scriptures against the Devil: He simply quoted the Scriptures and defended His position – He never attacked. Thus, those who use the Bible to cut and stab other people are wrong on two counts. It was the yet carnal Peter who used the sword to slash the man's ear off but it was Christ Who stuck the ear back on again (Luke 22:50-51). It was on the same occasion that Jesus warned that "all who take the sword will perish by the sword" (Matthew 26:52). Those who use the Bible as a sword to maim, kill and attack are declaring that they are more like the carnal Peter than the Savior. In the process of using the sword offensively, they open themselves to die by the same means they choose to live.

Neither does the end justify the means. It does not matter how noble your cause may be – if you go about it in an un-Christ-like and carnal way you will not have the Lord's blessing but will rather fall afoul of His judgment. "For with what judgment you judge, you will be judged; and with the measure you use, it will be measured back to you" (Matthew 7:2) and "judgment is without mercy to the one who has shown no mercy" (James 2:13).

Now before you accuse me of saying that we should not stand for Truth against error – that is not what I am saying. We must contend for the faith, defend the Gospel and point out error. But the attitude and method with which we do so are of utmost importance. Yes, just as important as the what is the how. We must speak the Truth, but we must do so with love (Ephesians 4:15).

I am afraid that I see only a few who speak the Truth, but of those few most speak the Truth with hate, anger, bitterness, arrogance and vindictiveness. It does not matter how much Truth you speak; if you do so with the wrong attitude you are wasting your time. The Lord will not honor you and He will not bless your words. 1Corinthians 13 is abundantly clear that it does not matter how great your (Bible) knowledge, how much you speak, how many books or articles you have written, or what sacrifices you have made – even to martyrdom. If you have not been driven by a love for those you address, you have wasted your time and you are just another big noise and irritation.

What is it that motivates you to defend the Truth? Some do so out of a love for themselves, and others because they love to be right and love to prove how wrong others are. The only legitimate motivation is love for the Lord Jesus, love for His Word and love for those who are lost. If you are not motivated by a love for all three, you are wasting everyone's time – rather get into politics or something else, but forget about speaking for the Lord Jesus. Unless we love what He loves, and hate what He hates, we have no right to speak on His behalf. Yes, He does hate error, but He hates arrogance even more, and He loves the sinner and the heretic. Until we genuinely love and weep for the heretics, we have no right to speak to or about them. How dare we claim to represent the One who laid down His life for us when we are more interested in proving how right we are than saving those who are lost and going astray?

CHAPTER 2

ARGUMENTATIVE OR CONTENDING?

"Hold fast the pattern of sound words which you have heard from me, in faith and love which are in Christ Jesus" - 2 TIMOTHY 1:13

SPEAKING AND DEFENDING THE Truth are some of the most important responsibilities of the church, its leaders, and all believers. There are many who propagate error and there are only a few who stand for doctrinal purity. But we must contend for the faith by the right method and with the right attitude. To this end, Paul provides some very clear instructions:

We are to "avoid foolish and ignorant disputes, knowing that they generate strife" (2 Timothy 2:23). This does not only apply to our relationship with those who are likeminded but especially to those who are of a different persuasion. Obviously we do not have disputes with those who believe like we do – the disputes are with those with whom we disagree. The context also makes it clear that this instruction applies when we relate to "those who are in opposition" (2 Timothy 2:23) and with those who have been entrapped by the devil (v 26).

It is important to note that most of the proof texts that are used as an excuse for a harsh attitude such as Titus 1:13 ("rebuke them sharply") and 1Timothy 5:20 ("Those who are sinning rebuke in the presence of all") are applicable in the context of the local assembly. When discipline is exercised in the local church, it is always tempered with love and with the purpose of winning the sinner and protecting the flock. When these verses are taken out of this context and applied on the Internet or in print, the rebuke is not balanced by the prayers, love and concern of a local body. They thus become inflammatory and lead to animosity, rather than healing and restoration. The same happens when local leaders choose to write a letter to the offender rather than speaking to them face-to-face (Matthew 18:15).

Sometimes I think that many people who get into apologetic type ministries do so simply because they love an argument. Even if that was not what got them into this kind of work, it seems to be what motivates them. Many just love the excitement of the scrap, and they get their kicks out of proving how right they are and how wrong others are. I know a few who will disagree with anything one says – just to pick an argument. (If you are irritated by this writing, you may well be one of these.) Others enjoy the fact that engaging in debate makes them feel intellectual, while others just must have the last word. Then there are those who have to win every argument and who, like bulldogs, cannot release once their jaws have locked onto the prey.

Paul is specific: we are to avoid those arguments that lead to strife. Even as I write, I know someone is rushing to remind me that Paul refers to "foolish and ignorant disputes" and that arguments about the Truth cannot be "foolish and ignorant." The fact is that it is the process of dispute or argument itself that is foolish and ignorant, not the subject. On several occasions, Paul warns Timothy not to argue over words and the Law, but rather to concentrate on things that are edifying: "Nor give heed to fables and endless genealogies, which cause disputes rather than godly edification which is in faith" (1Timothy 1:4). "But reject profane and old wives' fables, and exercise yourself toward godliness" (1 Timothy 4:7).

In 1Timothy 6:4-5, Paul links this argumentative attitude with pride. He instructs Titus to do the same: "But avoid foolish disputes, genealogies, contentions, and strivings about the law; for they are unprofitable and useless. Reject a divisive man after the first and second admonition, knowing that such a person is warped and sinning, being self-condemned" (Titus 3:9-11). This does not mean that we should not defend the Truth, nor even take a strong position against error. The problem Paul is addressing is the argumentative spirit, which is often a sign of immaturity. In 2 Timothy 2:22-23, Paul links argumentativeness with youthful lusts since it is the younger men who tend to love the fights. Maturity in Christ should bring a meekness and wisdom that restrains the carnal instinct to fight.

The Scribes loved to squabble. Their whole lives centered around argument, debate and questioning. They often tried to engage Jesus in endless arguments, but Jesus knew better than waste His time arguing with people who were not really interested in the Truth. He would exchange a few questions with them, but would quickly close the discussion by honing in on a very important flaw in their argument or by pointing out the hypocrisy in their statements.

Jesus would spend endless hours teaching His disciples and others who really wanted to know the Truth. He was infinitely patient with the sinners, the weak and the genuine "seekers." Yet He had no time to waste on those who were arrogant, self-seeking and opinionated. One of the most important skills we need is to discern between those who really want to know the Truth and those who are simply seeking an endorsement for their own theories or justification for their error.

It seems to me that we often forget that our calling is not to win arguments, but to teach, make disciples, and clearly define the Truth for those who are disciples or really want to be disciples. Many Christians will spend endless hours arguing with Jehovah's Witnesses and atheists, knowing full well that the other person is not really interested in the Truth. It is simply a waste of time. For example, I think it was Josh MacDowell who teaches to ask the evolutionist or atheist the following question: "If I can prove that God exists and that He created all things, would you believe on Him and surrender your life to Him?" Most of the time the response will be "No."

So, then, what is the purpose of a protracted argument if the other party is not really interested in knowing the Truth (The

Person)? There is no point – don't waste your time. Rather give him the Gospel as clearly and logically as possible and leave it there. In most instances the other person will be quite happy to be rid of you by now. The hypocrites did not stick around to debate Jesus on the intricacies of the Law after he said: "He who is without sin among you, let him throw a stone at her first" (John 8:7).

It seems to me that the difference between Jesus and us is that everything He said was led by the Spirit, while we often respond out of our fleshly desires to prove ourselves. If only we could be led by the Spirit on every occasion to discern whether we are dealing with an honest seeker of Truth or not. It is more important that we be led by the Spirit to say the right things, and to stop arguing before we begin to war in the flesh against the flesh. But it is even more important that we exhibit the right attitude of meekness, humility and wisdom.

Please take a few minutes to consider whether the wisdom you often display is true, heavenly wisdom, or the false, earthly and demonic wisdom:

"Who is wise and understanding among you? Let him show by good conduct that his works are done in the meekness of wisdom. But if you have bitter envy and self-seeking in your hearts, do not boast and lie against the Truth. This wisdom does not descend from above, but is earthly, sensual, demonic. For where envy and self-seeking exist, confusion and every evil thing are there. But the wisdom that is from above is first pure, then peaceable, gentle, willing to yield, full of mercy and good fruits, without partiality and without hypocrisy. Now the fruit of righteousness is sown in peace by those who make peace" (James 3:13-18).

Indeed, both arguments may appear wise and clever and both may even be founded on the Bible, but one is Godly and one is demonic.

CHAPTER 3

DO NOT QUARREL

"...avoid foolish and ignorant disputes, knowing that they generate strife. And a servant of the Lord must not quarrel but be gentle to all, able to teach, patient, in humility correcting those who are in opposition, if God perhaps will grant them repentance, so that they may know the Truth, and that they may come to their senses and escape the snare of the devil, having been taken captive by him to do his will." - 2 TIMOTHY 2:23-26

THESE VERSES ARE A clear and unequivocal command: The servant of the Lord is to avoid disputes and must not quarrel, but be gentle to all. There are no exceptions, ifs or buts. It does not say we are not to quarrel except with those who are heretics, and only be gentle to those who agree with us. We are not to quarrel. Period. We are to be gentle to ALL, including the heretics and "those who are in opposition."

I know that some will quote various other Scriptures on what Jesus and Paul may have done. But these verses Timothy are a direct command to us, equal to the Ten Commandments or any other direct command in the New

Testament. Those who claim that the Bible sanctions ungracious, vindictive and rude behavior are blatantly disobedient to this very clear instruction. Such disobedience places them at the same level as those whose doctrine they condemn. They choose to ignore certain Scriptures and to emphasize others, exactly the same thing that those with the bad attitude and "right" doctrine do. We had better "cast out the beam" from our own eye first (Matthew 7:3-5).

It is important to note, however that the injunction to "... avoid foolish and ignorant disputes... [to] not quarrel but be gentle to all..." is specifically to the "servant of the Lord." Those who ignore these verses must therefore disqualify themselves from being servants of the Lord.

Paul lists four aspects of our attitude that need to be in place when we try to correct someone else's doctrine. We will cover the first three in this chapter:

1) First, we are to be gentle to all. For "gentle" some expositors use the word "like a baby," meaning that we should be harmless, without guile, and as gentle as a baby would be! The Greek word for "gentle" in this passage is also used by Paul to describe his attitude to the Thessalonians: "we were gentle among you, just as a nursing mother cherishes her own children" (1 Thessalonians 2:7). That's right – Paul expects us to display the same kind of gentleness towards those who are in opposition as a mother does towards her baby! Yes, I know that is very far from what many do, but this is the clear teaching of the Word. The reason for this lies in verses 26 and 27 which I will explain later.

2) Second, Paul expects us to be "able to teach." This is the same requirement he places on those who wish to be overseers in the church: "A bishop must be... apt to teach" (1Timothy 3:2). There is a huge difference between those who are skilled in teaching and those who know many facts. Someone who is skilled at teaching educates others. One cannot be a teacher without ever coming face-to-face with students, learners or disciples. You cannot be a teacher in a vacuum, your study, or your academic ivory tower. You can only be a teacher when you impart wisdom (not just knowledge) to disciples.

Unfortunately, it has been my observation that many (not all) who get involved in apologetics ministries are not skilled at teaching. They live in isolation since they believe that they alone have the Truth. People like this often find it hard to relate to other people, let alone impart wisdom to others. Thus many of them sit in their glass houses, discern error and point fingers at those around them.

Let me be very clear on this: No one who is not involved in a local church (no matter how small), and who does not regularly teach the Truth, has the right to teach against error! There is no mention of a fault-finding, or critical ministry in the Bible. It is those who are "apt to teach" the Truth, who also then point out the error and warn concerning the wolves.

The reason for this is that daily interface with others, especially weak believers, helps to keep us humble, dependent on the Holy Spirit and in touch with the real issues of Christian living. There is nothing like relating to the weaknesses, problems and challenges of "normal" Christians to keep our ministries out of the area of theory and the academic. And there is nothing like the difficulty of imparting Biblical Truth to struggling believers to keep us aware of our own frailty and dependence on the Lord.

Every spectator on the sidelines of a sports game knows better how to play the game than anyone on the field! Yet there is no room for armchair critics in the church – only for those who are willing to roll up their sleeves and get their hands dirty with the vomit and diapers of new babes.

3) Thirdly we are to be "patient." Most commentators say of "patient" that it means to be "patient of ills and wrongs, forbearing" and "putting up with evil." That does not mean we must condone or accept wrongs and evil but, rather, that we should be patient with those who are wrong. This goes with the previous point on being apt to teach.

One of the most important skills in teaching is patience since many disciples are slow to learn and often make mistakes. Patience is even more necessary when dealing with those who are in error since it takes a long time to turn a ship around that is on the wrong course. Teaching babes is relatively easy as they are often a "blank slate" on which we can simply write the Truth. But when dealing with those who are in error, we must first delete the error before we can begin to write the Truth. This takes much more patience than teaching spiritual babes. If you do not have the patience to teach young Christians, then you will also not have the patience to correct those who are into error.

Let me emphasize again: I am not condoning error or heresy, neither am I unaware of the enormous damage false teachers have done and are doing. But unless we go about the task of defending the Truth in a godly way, we are wasting our time since the Lord will not support our efforts.

CHAPTER 4

CONTENDING WITH ATTITUDE

"But foolish and unlearned questions avoid, knowing that they do gender strifes. And the servant of the Lord must not strive; but be gentle unto all men, apt to teach, patient. In meekness instructing those that oppose themselves; if God peradventure will give them repentance to the acknowledging of the Truth; And that they may recover themselves out of the snare of the devil, who are taken captive by him at his will." - 2 TIMOTHY 2:23-26 KJV

IN THE PREVIOUS CHAPTER we looked at the first three aspects of the attitude of those who wish to bring correction to those who are in opposition. These are gentleness, an ability to teach and patience.

The fourth essential is humility or meekness. (Most translations use the word "gentleness" or "meekness"). Meekness is an aspect of the fruit of the Spirit listed in Galatians 5:23. It is not weakness but flows from a life which is fully surrendered to the will of God. Those who strive in their own strength, trying to establish their own purposes, are not meek, but are constantly agitated, arrogant, aggressive and antagonistic. Jonah is the best example of such a man. Paul before his conversion was also such, and the Lord described him as kicking against the goads (see Acts 9:5; 26:14).

Those who are meek have recognized their own weaknesses, are broken before Him, and have come to a point of full surrender to the Lord. They do not have to prove anything but are simply instruments in the hands of the Almighty.

Meekness flows first from an awareness of God's mercy towards us and a recognition of the fact that He has saved and kept us by His grace alone: "Put them in mind to… speak evil of no man, to be no brawlers, but gentle, shewing all meekness unto all men. For we ourselves also were sometimes foolish, disobedient, deceived, serving divers lusts and pleasures, living in malice and envy, hateful, and hating one another" (Titus 3:1-3 KJV).

Secondly, meekness flows from an awareness of our own faults and potential for sin and error. Those who arrogantly strive with others act as though they themselves never make mistakes and as though they have all truth: "Brethren, if a man be overtaken in a fault, ye which are spiritual, restore such an one in the spirit of meekness; considering thyself, lest thou also be tempted… For if a man think himself to be something, when he is nothing, he deceiveth himself" (Galatians 6:1,3 KJV).

Thirdly, meekness is a result of recognizing that we cannot change other people's minds, theology or attitudes. It is God alone who can do so (with the individual's cooperation). When we are deluded and overconfident and think that we can win the argument, prove how wrong the other person is, and get him to change his thinking – we are arrogant and far from meek. This is typical of the schoolyard bully who twists his opponent's arm behind his back, forcing him to submit. Spouses do the same in marriage when they have not yet learned that there is not a single person on this earth who can change the heart, mind or attitude of someone else. God alone has that power.

Those who are in opposition (to the Truth) are "in the snare of the devil, having been taken captive by him to do his will" (2Timothy 2:26). They are not free agents to change their minds as they choose, but are trapped in a web of deceit, lies and error. (How they got there is another story.) According to the Bible they are imprisoned and bound. To get angry with such people is a waste of time; they sold their freedom for expediency, fame or money. They cannot change unless the Lord intervenes. When we understand that, our attitude towards them has to change from one of judgment to one of pity and mercy.

Why did Jesus not debate Pilate? Surely He could prove His innocence and the illegality of the trial. Yet, He said nothing. The key lies in Jesus' words to Pilate: "You could have no power at all against Me unless it had been given you from above" (John 19:11). Jesus recognized where the true power lay. Those who fight with men have forgotten that "we do not wrestle against flesh and blood, but against principalities, against powers, against the rulers of the darkness of this age, against spiritual hosts of wickedness in the heavenly places" (Ephesians 6:12).

This does not mean that we should just sit back and wait for things to happen. The Lord uses men to work as His co-workers. Some of us plant, others water but the Lord gives the increase – and unless He does, nothing will happen in the lives of others. "Unless the Lord builds the house, they labor in vain who build it; Unless the Lord guards the city, the watchman stays awake in vain" (Psalm 127:1).

In dealing with those in error, we need to give a sound, logical and reason for the Truth. We need to be skilled workmen who divide the Word correctly. But the rest is up to the Lord: "...if God perhaps will grant them repentance, so that they may know the Truth, and that they may come to their senses and escape the snare of the devil" (2Timothy 2:25).

We cannot demand that God must deliver them, or that He has to honor our word and cause the seed to grow. Paul uses the word "perhaps/peradventure" indicating that it is entirely up to God. Having sown the seed, we need to leave the rest up to Him. He has to give them repentance. Once they find repentance, then they will know the Truth. Once they know the Truth they need to come to their senses and escape the Devil's trap. Sadly, many do come to know the Truth, but choose to stay in the snare of the Devil for the same reasons they were entrapped in the first place.

Thus we have three people in the equation: The speaker of Truth, God, and the individual in error. Even if the first two do everything necessary, the person in error may still choose to remain in bondage. The speaker of Truth is only one third of the equation, and we must understand and accept that we cannot control, manipulate, cajole or force people to change.

Our true attitude and motive is often revealed when people choose to continue in error, even when they have been given Truth. Only those who weep and mourn for those who choose to continue in error have the right to speak in the first place. Those who hurl accusations, malign, slander, and feel a sense of justification have no right to speak.

Should we, then, not point out error and name those who propagate error? What about Jesus cleansing the temple and His comments about the Pharisees? I will get to these questions in the next chapter; but for now, let's check our attitude. Are we speaking from a heart of brokenness, humility, love, compassion and pity? Or from a platform of pride and superiority – "God, I thank You that I am not like other men – extortioners, unjust, adulterers, or even as this tax collector" (Luke 18:12)?

CHAPTER 5

THE TRUTH WITH BROKENNESS

"A servant of the Lord must not quarrel but be gentle to all." - 2 TIMOTHY 2:23

THIS VERSE SEEMS TO contradict the fact that Jesus called the Pharisees a "brood of vipers" (Matthew 23:33), Herod "that fox" (Luke 13:32), and that He cleansed the temple and overturned the tables of the money changers.

These Scriptures are often used to support the malicious name-calling, animosity, insults and threats of those in apologetics-type ministries towards those in error. But do Jesus' actions contradict Paul's teaching, and do we have the right, even responsibility, to be aggressive and abrasive in our defense of the Truth?

First we have no instruction to act abusively, maliciously and uncouthly in our relating to others. In fact, we have clear instructions to not be malicious in our dealings, even with our enemies. Jesus said "...love your enemies, bless those who curse you, do good to those who hate you, and pray for those who spitefully use you and persecute you" (Matthew 5:44). He also said we must turn the other cheek (Luke 6:29).

Paul teaches: "Bless those who persecute you; bless and do not curse... repay no one evil for evil... do not avenge yourselves, but rather give place to wrath; for it is written, 'Vengeance is Mine, I will repay,' says the Lord. Therefore If your enemy is hungry, feed him; If he is thirsty, give him a drink; For in so doing you will heap coals of fire on his head. Do not be overcome by evil, but overcome evil with good" (Romans 12:14,17,19-21).

Concerning potential teachers James says: "Out of the same mouth proceed blessing and cursing. My brethren, these things ought not to be so. Does a spring send forth fresh water and bitter from the same opening? Can a fig tree, my brethren, bear olives, or a grapevine bear figs? Thus no spring yields both salt water and fresh" (James 3:10-12).

Peter reminds us that Jesus, "when He was reviled, did not revile in return; when He suffered, He did not threaten, but committed Himself to Him who judges righteously" (1Peter 2:23).

Peter further instructs us: "...not returning evil for evil or reviling for reviling, but on the contrary blessing... Let him seek peace and pursue it... And who is he who will harm you if you become followers of what is good? But even if you should suffer for righteousness' sake, you are blessed. "And do not be afraid of their threats, nor be troubled." (1Peter 3:9,11,13,14).

The writers of the New Testament are agreed that our attitude towards those who are outside the faith, even our enemies and the enemies of the Gospel should be one of love. Clearly, we are not to fellowship with them nor invite them into our homes, let alone our churches (1Timothy 6:5, 2John 1:10). Yet, our attitude towards them should be one of love since we are not the ones who will execute judgment or vengeance.

There are no contradictions in the Scriptures and, therefore, Jesus could not have acted inconsistently with the clear teaching of the Bible or with His purpose.

Jesus' actions are normally explained by the term "righteous indignation" or "righteous anger." I am sure that is what it was. He was angry. When someone becomes angry there are two important considerations: the motive and the actions. Jesus' anger was one hundred percent for the right reasons. His motives were not tinged by even the slightest bit of personal vendetta, pride, or any other wrong attitude. Neither did a single one of His actions not fully reflect the will of the Father.

So the questions we have to ask when we want to lash out at others who we think are heretics are:

1) Are my motives perfectly pure? Is there absolutely no sense of personal vendetta, trying to prove myself, pride, malice, nor any other motive that is contrary to the Word? Am I totally driven by a zeal for God's house and the Truth? Or, is there something else behind my attitude?

2) Do I act exactly in obedience to the will of God? When saying what I say about the wolves, do I reflect the Father, and do I say and do only what He commands?

Friends, after many years of observing (and participating with) those who go on major rants and tirades against the false teachers, I am convinced that the motive and the actions very seldom reflect the will of the Father, and that the tirades seldom glorify Him, but rather the speaker/writer.

Those of us who are defenders of the faith have two responsibilities in the area of false doctrine: Our first duty is to protect the sheep from error (Acts 20:28-31). Our second responsibility is to attempt to win the gainsayers (Titus 1:9, 2Timothy 2:25,26, Acts 18:21). (It seems that many are not doing either, but are rather trying to show how right they are and how wrong others are – for this they have no biblical mandate.) We do not protect the sheep any better by ranting and raving. On the contrary, we make some folk wonder why we protest so much. We certainly do not win any heretics to the Truth by slander, name-calling and venom. Thus neither aspect of our purpose is served by antagonism and rough words.

Should we then not name names and expose those who lead weak disciples astray? No, we must name names. Jesus, Paul, Peter and John all named names. Every writer of the New Testament exposed error and warned against error. This is a very important part of the mission of any true teacher of Truth. Unfortunately, unless the names are mentioned, people often do not make the connection between the false doctrine and the face on the television. Weak and new believers especially need to be given guidelines as to who is "kosher" and who is not. But, with what attitude do we name the heretics? Is it with glee and pride that we are not like so-and-so?

Or is it with sorrow over the need to even have to mention another's name in warning?

Matthew 23 is often quoted as an excuse to rail against others. In this chapter Jesus warns against the Pharisees, exposing them for all their falseness and error. Eight times He pronounces woe over them. He calls them whitewashed tombs, snakes, hypocrites, blind, fools and a few other things. Yes, He did all that – but with what attitude? I have seen many men do what Jesus did in the first 36 verses of that chapter. I have even heard a few apply verses 38 and 39. But I have never seen one of these people do what Jesus did in verse 37 of the same chapter. He wept and lamented over the same men that He was lambasting: "O Jerusalem, Jerusalem, the one who kills the prophets and stones those who are sent to her! How often I wanted to gather your children together, as a hen gathers her chicks under her wings, but you were not willing!" (Matthew 23:37). Many have styled themselves after the aggressive prophets of the Old Testament without bothering to see that the private moments of these brave men were filled with tears and heartache for the state of Israel.

Only when we are willing to season our insults with tears from a broken heart for the heretics do we have the right to say anything to them..

CHAPTER 6

AGAINST ERROR OR FOR TRUTH?

"You shall know the truth, and the truth shall make you free." - JOHN 8:32

WE HAVE LOOKED AT the motives, manners and methods we need to employ if we are going to stand against error. But maybe the question we should have begun with was whether standing against error is, in fact, a legitimate ministry, and whether or not there is any sanction in the Bible for a ministry to be built around standing against error.

Many think that standing against error and standing for the Truth are synonymous. Sadly, they are not. In standing for the Truth, we will of necessity stand against error. But those who stand against error do not necessarily stand for the Truth.

There are many who describe themselves in negatives: "We are not... We do not... We do not believe...." They do not know the Truth other than in terms of what it is not. Some of these dear brothers cannot preach a single message or write a single word unless "inspired" by some error. So, if you are a preacher, teacher or writer, let me ask you this question: When preparing to write or to speak, do you think in terms of what you are going to speak against, or in terms of the Truth you wish to instill in the lives of the hearers?

A careful examination of the words of the Apostles preached in the book of Acts will not reveal a single message designed to disprove any other religion or refute any error but, rather, every message was a very clear and positive declaration of Truth. "And daily in the temple, and in every house, they ceased not to teach and preach Jesus Christ" (Acts 5:42). Jesus did not say that we will see the error and so be set free from it. He did say: "You shall know the truth, and the truth shall make you free" (John 8:32).

Those who stand against error often fall into an equal but opposite error to the one they oppose. Their theology is reactive since they do not form their theology based on a study of the Scriptures but, rather, their doctrine is shaped by a reaction to what is wrong. Ephesians 4:14 speaks of "children, tossed to and fro and carried about with every wind of doctrine." Have you ever noticed a tree or man "tossed to and fro" by the wind? The wind only blows in one direction, yet sometimes the person will fall – not in the direction that the wind is blowing, but into the wind. Why? Because they over-corrected.

In the same way, winds of doctrine toss the immature "to and fro." While some are just "carried about with every wind of doctrine" others will overreact to it and fall in the opposite direction. This is just like when the opposing team in tug-a-war suddenly stops pulling and the other team falls down. Thus, people open themselves to be manipulated by the Devil into an opposite but equal, and sometimes greater, error.

Did you know that almost none of the errors of early Roman church came about as a result of a lack of diligence or commitment to the Truth, but that almost all of their many heresies can be traced back to an effort to stand against some error and to protect the church? Broadbent, in his excellent history of the church titled The Pilgrim Church, says: "The means adopted to counter these attacks and to preserve unity of doctrine affected the church even more than the heresies themselves" (p. 30). There are countless examples of churches and individuals holding to some error simply because they overreacted to a bad experience in their past.

Experiential theology is wrong when it is based on someone's positive or negative experience and not on the Bible. The fact that someone was healed by standing on his head is not a reason to incorporate head-standing into one's doctrine. We must base our doctrine on the clear teaching of the Word of God. In the same way we cannot allow the many errors and abuses out there to shape our thinking or preaching even one little bit. Our values, doctrine and views must be based on the Word, and on the Word alone.

I am all for pointing out error. By simply preaching against various errors we may well equip people to see one specific error. But people will likely fall for the next error if it has not been defined for them. Sadly, many folk who know everything about heresies do not know the Truth. And they might even mistakenly categorize pure doctrine as error since they do not know how to recognize the Truth when they come across it.

We must equip people to know the Truth. If we know the Truth, we will recognize error in every disguise. I'm sure you have heard the story about people who are trained to detect counterfeit money by first being trained to recognize the real thing. Once they know the real they can easily detect the fake. (I did some research and this is true.)

Error is like the viruses that attack our computers. I once heard that every day 65 new viruses are unleashed. It is impossible to keep a complete list of the latest threats against your computer, let alone against your soul. A far better approach is for people to know the Truth and, thus, be able to recognize that which is not Truth by comparing it to what is Truth.

The plumbline (Amos 7:7,8) does not contain a copy of everything that can be wrong with a wall. It simply shows a true vertical line; and when the plumbline is dropped, and the wall compared to it, every flaw in the wall becomes evident.

More than teaching people doctrinal Truth, we must bring them into a relationship with The Truth - Jesus Christ. And The Truth (Jesus Christ) will set them free. It is no good collecting various truths if we do not have The Truth. One of the questions I am often asked is how will we recognize the Antichrist? The answer is simple: Know the real Christ and you will recognize the impostor.

In the past 30 years, millions of people have been caught up by many dozens of heresies, taught by charlatans who have proliferated in the wake of the Charismatic Renewal Movement. If only the deceived knew the Bible, and knew their God, they would never have been misled. Yet, over the years we have seen many people come to the Light and turn from error, simply by being taught the whole Truth. The Word is powerful! And if only we will – in humility, with clean hands – break it open and share it with folks, many will be set free and come into true fellowship with the Father and the Son.

The purpose of the Word, and the preaching and teaching of the Word, is "that the man of God may be complete, thoroughly equipped for every good work" (2Timothy 3:16). Are we equipping people for good work? If not, we are missing the mark, even when preaching the Truth.

CHAPTER 7

WATCHMAN OR GOSSIP?

"Son of man, I have made you a watchman." - EZEKIEL
3:17

FOR YEARS THE EVIL King Saul pursued David like a man does
an animal. He tried to kill him many times, broke David's marriage,
and caused him to live the life of a vagabond and a fugitive. There is
not any good to be said for Saul and, by all estimations, the sooner
he died and David ascended to the throne the better for the nation.

One day Saul did die. The young Amalekite man who
assisted in Saul's suicide ran to bring David the good news and the
crown he had taken from Saul's corpse. He thought David would be
glad to hear that his tormentor was dead so that David could finally
claim the throne. But instead David mourned for Saul, rent his
clothes, and sang a lament over the death of the king and Jonathan
(2Samuel 1). The young man who killed Saul and who carried the
news was executed for his trouble. David says of the event: "When
someone told me, saying, 'Look, Saul is dead,' thinking to have
brought good news, I arrested him and had him executed in Ziklag –

the one who thought I would give him a reward for his news" (2Samuel 4:10).

A little while later David's spoiled son Absalom stirred a revolt against David, went to war against the king, and tried to kill his own father. When David heard the news that the rebellion was quelled and that Absalom was killed, he again mourned rather than rejoiced (2Samuel 18, 19). These are some examples of how a godly man reacts to the news of the fall of the wicked. Even Samuel, who never wanted to anoint Saul as King, mourned at Saul's failure (1Samuel 15:35).

How do we react to the news of the fall of Christians, or to the rumor of the latest heresy that comes out of the camp of the false teachers? Do we take delight in pouncing on the latest tidbit of scandal and spreading it as wide as possible? Or do we react like David and Samuel did?

In many parts of the world tow trucks can be seen waiting at busy intersections. In our family we refer to them as "vultures" since they hang around waiting to feed on someone else's misfortune. In America they are often referred to as "ambulance chasers." To wait for and profit from someone else's hurt has to be one of the lowest forms of human existence. While the tow truck driver and the vulture have some purpose, any form of scavenger, as well as those who handle the dead, are declared unclean under the Law. The young man who brought the news to David was an Amalekite. The Amalekites were always waiting in the wings to profit off Israel's weak moments and are referred to as "the people against whom the Lord will have indignation forever" (Malachi 1:4).

Jesus and Satan stand at two opposites. Satan is the accuser of the brethren (Revelation 12:10). Jesus, on the other hand, "makes intercession for the saints" (Romans 8:27). Thus, those who accuse support the ministry of Satan, while those who enter into the ministry of Jesus grieve and mourn, and make intercession for those who sin and fall.

Watchmen who warn about impending danger have an important role throughout the Bible (Ezekiel 3:17, Acts 20:28-31). But, there is a huge difference between a watchman and a gossip. A watchman takes no delight in reporting the threat, while the gossip enjoys telling and re-telling the juicy stories of sin and failure. These gossips are just like the godless Athenians who "spent their time in nothing else but either to tell or to hear some new thing" (Acts 17:21). Some who style themselves as "defenders of the faith" take extreme delight in rehearsing the latest error. I have seen the glint in their eye as they play the latest DVD, or as they sit around the table seeking to tell of some greater error than the previous speaker. Some rush to the computer keyboard to publish the latest juicy morsel as quickly and as widely as possible.

Is this the spirit of Christ or of Satan? Is this how King David would have reacted?

Even worse, like sharks who have smelled blood, many rush in for the kill without even checking if the rumor is true or false or, worse, determine if the accused is friend or foe. Thus they begin to feed on one another. It is very sad when anyone dies in war, and when innocent bystanders die it is a tragedy. But there are no words to describe the horror, injustice and catastrophe of someone killed by "friendly fire." Paul warns that "if you bite and devour one another, beware lest you be consumed by one another!" (Galatians 5:15).

The Scriptures (Old and New) are clear that "two or three witnesses" are required to make an accusation stick. (See Deuteronomy 17:6, Matthew 18:6, and 1Timothy 5:19.) Even in the world one is not allowed to brand someone a criminal unless he has been found guilty in court; yet we Christians will accuse and execute another based on a single rumor. That makes us no different to those who conspired to crucify Jesus without any evidence of wrongdoing. (Please note that I am not against dealing appropriately with heretics, schismatics and immoral leaders, but let's get the facts first.)

Timing is critical when dealing with someone in error. It is only natural for us to rush in, guns blazing as we deal with perceived error or sin. Yet, Paul says we need to be patient. "A servant of the Lord must not quarrel but be gentle to all, able to teach, patient" (2Timothy 2:24). We need to be patient, because there is a right and a wrong time to deal with every matter. Many times God is already at work and if we just give Him a little time, He Himself will bring repentance and correction. The Lord may already be using someone else to minister to the situation. But, because of our arrogance we feel that God is dependent on us, and if we don't sort things out immediately God's whole Kingdom will be destroyed. Once again those who tend to shoot first and ask questions later have never served in a local church. It is in the local church that we learn to wait for the Lord's timing, and learn that He often sorts things out Himself, before we can mess them up.

Here is one of many examples that I have personally witnessed, where the gung-ho attitude of a discernment worker caused more damage than healing: A small assembly in a very small town was having difficulties. Some of the leaders were teaching a few things contrary to Scripture. At the same time, local brothers were ministering to the situation and were on the verge of a break-through when a travelling preacher rode into town. The foreigner heard part of the story and opened fire without further investigation. When he rode out of town a few days later a church, and the Lord's name, lay broken in the dust. The only evangelical church in the town was split, and instead of a single healthy church, the town ended with several factions. Families were destroyed, friendships broken, ministries ruined, and the credibility of the Gospel may never be restored in the eyes of the unbelievers of that community.

Why?

Some do this for personal profit. Money is made out of books, tapes and speaking tours exposing the latest sins. Authors and speakers need to strike first since no one wants old news. Others need the scalps to feed their egos. And sadly, others just love the "excitement" of the kill! God help us! Are we any better than the tabloid press? I don't think so. Some preachers will build a following of "disciples" who hang on their every word, who support them financially, feed their egos and encourage the preacher to expose even more lurid details. When these preachers cannot dish fresh dirt, some of them are not beyond inventing things, exaggerating or even blowing a minor incident into a full-blown event.

Preoccupation with sin, error or deception has a negative impact on the person so engaged. Before 1994, South Africa had a censorship board that viewed and censored every movie that came into the country. Several of these men were preachers. I often wonder what impact all the smut must have had on the minds of these men. Sin, whether in the performance or the observation of it, has the same desensitizing and soiling effect on the doer as well as the spectator. Pornography is equally destructive to the audience and the performers. Thus, a preoccupation with heresy impacts the sensitivity of the heart of the one so occupied. This is why many become blind to their own sins and doctrinal shortcomings. Jesus warned about removing the log out of one's own eye before trying to remove the splint out of another's (Matthew 7:3-5).

Which is worse: the man who, for whatever reason, does not yet understand the Trinity, but who sincerely loves the Lord with all his heart and who walks humbly with his God? Or, the man who can write a treatise on the intricacies of the tri-unity of God, but who is bigoted, bitter, vengeful, proud, a divider of brethren and a gossip? I do not condone false doctrine, but we can have all the right teachings yet still have denied the essence of the Gospel.

The Ephesians had the right doctrine, hated those who were evil and were able to discern true apostles from the false. Yet, the Lord says they are fallen because they had left their first love (Revelation 2:1-7).

Love "does not rejoice in iniquity, but rejoices in the Truth" (1 Corinthians 13:6).

CHAPTER 8

KILLING THE MESSENGER

"Keep yourselves in the love of God, looking for the mercy of our Lord Jesus Christ unto eternal life. And of some have compassion, making a difference: And others save with fear, pulling them out of the fire; hating even the garment spotted by the flesh." - JUDE 21-23

IN CASE YOU GET the impression from what I have written so far that I am against any form of apologetics or discernment ministries – I am not. The ministry of a watchman is vitally important to the church. But, unfortunately, many have brought discredit to a crucial ministry by their bad attitude.

Even sadder than the fact that those with bad attitudes have brought disgrace to all who stand for the Truth, is the fact that these same "watchmen" often cannot receive correction from others. It seems they often regard themselves as being above correction and the only custodians of Truth. When someone dares bring balance or correction to them, they immediately turn their sword on the messenger, and seek to discount the Lord's messenger.

Some even feel that admonition is proof of the fact that they are "suffering for the faith." But the Scriptures are clear that it is only when our suffering is wholly for His sake that we can claim to be martyrs. When we suffer for our own bad attitude and misdeeds we only get what we deserve (1Peter 4:15, 3:16, 2:20). It seems to me that a lot of the attacks that come against "defenders of the faith" is deserved. And, sadly, nothing can repair the damage done by such loose cannons.

Those on both sides of the fence seem to find it hard to accept correction. Those who claim to be "defenders of the faith" should be more sensitive to correction than the heretics. Sadly, it seems that both sides equally resist the admonition of the Lord through His servants.

We would all find it very easy to receive rebuke if the Lord Jesus Himself appeared to us and spoke the words. But, He mostly chooses to speak through the most unlikely representatives. And because the message does not come in the package we expect it to, we reject it with contempt and often kill the messenger. We may not kill them physically, but we kill their reputations and sometimes their entire ministries.

God spoke to Israel through the thunder and the lightning. He spoke to Balaam through the ass, to Israel through unpopular prophets, and to the Jews through the social misfit clothed in camel skins called John. They were all rejected. When Jesus came as a carpenter's son, Nathaniel echoed the views of the nation when he said: "Can anything good come out of Nazareth?" (John 1:46; 7:41).

It seems that we humans are very good at finding a reason to reject and even kill the messenger (Matthew 23:37-39). Rather, we should be listening to hear the voice of the Shepherd who speaks and seeks our attention in the most unexpected ways.

Balaam became the archetype of a prophet gone wrong. Three times the New Testament refers to him as an evil example of a prophet for hire. But it was not always so. There was a time when he had a relationship with the living God, and when the Lord spoke to and through him (Numbers 22:9-13). So how did he sink so low as to actually advise the Moabites to commit adultery with the Children of Israel, and thus incur the wrath of God? By rejecting the message of the Lord. Numbers 22 records how it happened:

First the Lord spoke to him directly (v12) but the Word did not suit Balaam. This is the first step towards apostasy – rejecting the Word because it does not please us. This is why the seeker-friendly churches are packed and those who preach the Truth are empty – people simply do not want to hear a message that confronts them or their sin. Ahab had collected a retinue of prophets who all told him what he wanted to hear. But he despised the one man who told the Truth (1Kings 22). We all glibly accept that all our ways are pure (Proverbs 16:2) and cannot believe that anyone dare suggest otherwise. Apologist and heretic both claim immunity and infallibility under the banner of "the Lord's anointed."

As a result of Balaam's disobedience, and in a very short time, the donkey saw what the prophet could not (Numbers

22:23). How sad when even animals and children can see what we cannot. The donkey then turned out of the way. This was out of character and we should take heed to every event that comes our way that is out of the routine. It may just be the Lord's way of getting our attention. Instead we do just what Balaam did; we fix the problem with brute force. Rather, we should dismount and ask the Lord whether He is trying to get our attention.

Balaam beat the poor animal and got his own agenda back on track (v25). Soon after, the donkey crushed Balaam's foot against the wall. The pain should have gotten his attention. It is sad to watch people hurting because the Lord is trying to get their attention. But it is tragic to see them pull out the whip and beat the very thing that the Lord has used to address them. As a preacher I have tremendous sympathy for that poor donkey, having been on the receiving end of the same treatment many times.

Next the donkey lay down under Balaam. If we were to translate this into modern English it would read: "then the wheels came off." This time Balaam did not use the whip but took his staff to the poor animal in an attempt to kill it. (He wished the rod had been a sword.) How violent do we become towards those who are only trying to help us?! When the wheels come off our health, finances, relationships, ministry, etc., we need to take heed – it is very likely the Lord trying to get through to us.

In the end, the donkey spoke to Balaam in an audible voice. Surely that should have grabbed his attention, but still he would not listen. Yes, the Lord speaks through the most unlikely mouthpieces, but nothing gets the ear of those who do not want to hear. Balaam was angry with the very thing that the Lord had sent to save his life (v33). Whenever people react to the preaching or reading of the Word with anger it is a sure sign that they heard, but refused, to receive the message. How sad.

Finally the Angel of the Lord Himself appeared to him and spoke to him. Still he did not listen, but continued on his merry way. Five times the Lord tried to get his attention, but his continued disobedience, ambition and greed had made him deaf.

Do not despise the warnings because the instruments that bring them are not esteemed in your eyes. Listen, because the Lord speaks through the most unlikely people, events and things.

If this booklet has angered, confronted, convicted or been a reproach to you, please pray that the Lord may help you hear what it is He is trying to say. The fact that you have stayed with us through these pages is a good sign; but now you may need to ask for forgiveness for pride and for those you have hurt, slandered or even turned away from the Truth through an un-Christlike attitude. You need to seek the Lord's forgiveness first, and then the forgiveness of those you have wronged.

ENDNOTES

This *booklet* was originally published as part of a series of articles posted on the Herescope blog, a project of the Discernment Research Group.

Chapter 1:
http://herescope.blogspot.com/2007/06/contentiously-contending.html
Chapter 2:
http://herescope.blogspot.com/2007/06/argumentative-or-contending.html
Chapter 3:
http://herescope.blogspot.com/2007/06/not-to-quarrel.html
Chapter 4:
http://herescope.blogspot.com/2007/06/contending-with-attitude.html
Chapter 5:
http://herescope.blogspot.com/2007/07/Truth-with-brokenness.html
Chapter 6:
http://herescope.blogspot.com/2007/07/against-error-or-for-Truth.html
Chapter 7:
http://herescope.blogspot.com/2007/07/watchman-or-gossip.html
Chapter 8:
http://herescope.blogspot.com/2007/07/killing-messenger.html

Made in the USA
Lexington, KY
08 March 2016